The Library of Physics™

THE BASICS OF QUANTUM PHYSICS

Understanding the Photoelectric Effect and Line Spectra

Edward Willett

The Rosen Publishing Group, Inc., New York

This book is dedicated to the late Isaac Asimov, who helped to inspire my interest in science and science writing.

Published in 2005 by The Rosen Publishing Group, Inc.
29 East 21st Street, New York, NY 10010

Library of Congress Cataloging-in-Publication Data

Willett, Edward, 1959–
The basics of quantum physics: understanding the photoelectric effect and line spectra / by Edward Willett.
    p. cm.
Includes bibliographical references and index.
ISBN 1-4042-0334-6 (library binding)
1. Spectrum analysis. 2. Photoelectricity. 3. Quantum theory.
I. Title.
QC451.W55 2005
530.12—dc22

                                                    2004013652

Manufactured in the United States of America

On the cover: As two beams of white light pass through prisms, they are refracted. The light is split into its component wavelengths and produces a spectrum. Each spectrum is reflected by a mirror (which you cannot see in this picture) at the bottom corners.

Contents

Introduction

To some people, "quantum physics" is a scary phrase. It's become a shorthand expression for "extremely complicated," much like "rocket science." Although the details of quantum physics are certainly complex, and require more mathematical knowledge than most people possess, the basics of quantum physics can be grasped by just about anyone.

The classical physics of Sir Isaac Newton (1642–1727) lay at the heart of the scientific world-view in the nineteenth century. The first early steps into the astonishing new world of quantum physics took place in the early part of the twentieth century. In the span of a few short years, classical physics was overturned, at least for events at the subatomic level.

Those steps had to be taken because classical physics could not explain some of the phenomena scientists were seeing in their experiments. The end result was a whole new way of looking at the subatomic world, and a whole new understanding of the basic structure of the universe.

The prisms in the lens of the Portland Bill Lighthouse, on the southern tip of the Isle of Portland in England, split light as it passes through them. When white light passes through a prism, it is separated into an ordered arrangement of colors, which Sir Isaac Newton called a spectrum.

In this book, you'll learn how this new way of looking at the world came about. Specifically, you'll learn about two of the phenomena that classical physics could not explain, but that quantum physics could: the photoelectric effect and line spectra.

Today, scientists are still exploring the ramifications of quantum physics, which underpin everything from chemistry to cosmology. That's why it's important to understand the origins of quantum physics.

The Nature of Light

By the end of the eighteenth century, scientists knew that the visible world was made of invisible particles. They believed these particles, called atoms, obeyed clear physical laws. Sir Isaac Newton first spelled out these laws in his book *Principia*, which was published in 1687.

Scientists were so sure of their understanding that Pierre-Simon Laplace (1749–1827), a French physicist, claimed at the end of the eighteenth century that if you had unlimited calculating powers and complete knowledge of the position, mass, and velocity of all particles at any given moment, you could use Newton's equations to predict the future. But there were still a few little problems to solve. One was the nature of light. Newton had suggested that light might be made up of tiny particles, or what he called "corpuscles." After all, he reasoned, if matter was made up of particles—atoms—why shouldn't light be?

However, others had different ideas. Christian Huygens (1629–1695) of Holland, for instance, who lived at the same time as Newton, thought that perhaps light behaved more like a wave.

Sir Isaac Newton

Sir Isaac Newton (1642–1727) was one of the most important scientists who ever lived. His laws of gravitation and motion explained how objects move on Earth and in space. He established the science of optics—the study of the behavior of light—and built the first reflecting telescope. He invented calculus. Among his books are two of the greatest scientific works ever written: *Philosophiae Naturalis Principia Mathematica* (Mathematical Principles of Natural Philosophy), published in 1687, and *Opticks* (Optics), published in 1704.

Pictured here are Sir Isaac Newton's reflecting telescope, which he invented in 1668, and his manuscript entitled *Philosophiae Naturalis Principia Mathematica*. In *Principia*, he presented his three laws of motion and definitions for absolute space and time.

Particles vs. Waves

To understand why the nature of light mattered, it's important to understand the differences between a particle and a wave. Particles are easy to understand. A particle is essentially a discrete object. A baseball can be considered a particle; so can a child's building block. A particle occupies a single, localized volume of space. Its energy is all concentrated within that volume. If you have some means of observing a particle, you can say at any given moment precisely where it is and how (or whether) it is moving. A wave is quite different. A wave is a pattern of matter (or energy, or both), spread out over a volume of space. Waves are all around us. Waves on a lake or a sea are the most familiar examples. Those are water waves. A vibrating guitar string is a wave—a metal or nylon wave. Sound is an air wave.

There are a number of ways to measure waves. The wavelength is the distance between the highest points, or crests, of two successive waves. The frequency is how many waves pass a particular point in a certain amount of time. The amplitude is how much the wave varies from the normal level of the undisturbed medium: either the height of the crest or the depth of the lowest point, or trough. (In other

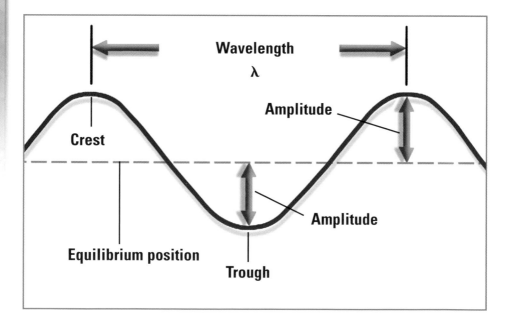

A wavelength is the distance between corresponding points on two successive waves. Each crest is one wavelength from the next crest, and each trough is one wavelength from the next trough. Wavelength is represented by the Greek letter lambda (λ).

words, the amplitude of a water wave on a lake is the height of the wave crests above or depths of the wave troughs below the surface level of the water on a perfectly still day.)

Unlike a particle, waves can be spread out over an immense area. A wave doesn't exist in a single location. Instead, it's everywhere its crests and troughs are.

So, which is light, a particle, or a wave?

Thomas Young's Experiment

In 1801, English physicist Thomas Young (1773–1829) came up with an experiment that produced some of the strongest evidence yet that light was wavelike. Young shone light from a single source onto a screen that had two narrow slits in it. The light shone through the slits onto another screen that Young had placed a little way behind the first.

Young reasoned that if light were made up of particles, then each particle should pass straight through one of the slits in the first screen and land on the second screen, creating two bright patches directly behind the slits. If, on the other hand, light were wavelike, it could be expected to spread out once it had passed through the slits. Waves in the ocean, after all, spread across a harbor after entering it through a narrow gap in the sea wall. If light were a wave, it should pass through the slits, then spread out on the second screen. Not only that, but

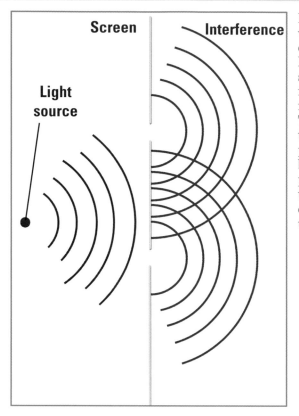

Screen

Interference

Light source

In this two-slit experiment, where light falls on two closely spaced slits, the light passing through each slit spreads out, or diffracts. The spreading light from the slits overlaps. Thomas Young discovered that the overlap created a pattern of bright and dark bands called interference patterns. He also reasoned that the patterns could be explained only by assuming that light travels as waves.

the light that passed through one slit would mingle with the light that passed through the other.

When two sets of waves mingle, the results depend on how the waves relate to each other. If they are perfectly in step, then the crests and troughs of one set of waves exactly match the crests and troughs of the other set of waves, creating extra-high waves. If they are perfectly out of step, then the crests of one set of waves correspond to the troughs of the second set of waves, and the waves cancel each other out, resulting in no apparent waves at all. If they are just slightly out of step, then you get what are called interference patterns: sometimes wave crests match up, and sometimes crests match up with troughs. If the waves in question are made of light, this should appear as alternating bands of light and darkness.

When Young shone his light through the two slits in the first screen, this is exactly what he saw on the second screen: alternating light and dark bands. It seemed to be unmistakable evidence that light came in waves, not particles.

Light as Electromagnetic Waves

As the century progressed, it became evident that light, electricity, and magnetism are all linked. Visible light was clearly just a narrow band of frequencies within a much larger spectrum of electromagnetic waves. (Different colors of light are simply light waves with different frequencies.) All electromagnetic waves traveled at the same speed—the speed of light, just under 300,000 kilometers per second. James Clerk Maxwell (1831–1879) published the equations that spell this out in 1873. These waves were believed to travel through a mysterious, invisible medium called the ether. Scientists believed the ether had to exist because they thought a wave has to travel through something; after all, you can't have an ocean wave without water, or a sound wave without air. In fact, there's no such thing as the ether. Electro-magnetic waves can travel through a vacuum.

With the realization that light was simply a kind of electromagnetic wave, many physicists thought that all the big ideas of physics were known. All that was left, it seemed, was a lot of tidying up of the details. "The future truths of physical science are to be looked for in the sixth place of decimals." In 1894, physicist Albert A. Michelson (1852–1931) put it this way.

In fact, as the nineteenth century drew toward its close, a young man in Germany by the name of Max Planck (1858–1947) was warned against going into physics. Physics, he was told, was at the end of its road. There was little worthwhile left to do in the field. Planck fortunately ignored the advice; in a few years he would play a central role in turning classical physics upside down and ushering in the age of quantum physics.

But for now, let's turn our attention away from light. At this point in the nineteenth century, after all, physicists thought they had that problem figured out. Instead, their attention was focused on something else they'd thought they had figured out but were now beginning to wonder about again: the atom.

The Nature of the Atom

The notion that everything is made up of tiny particles called atoms goes back to the ancient Greeks in the fifth century BC. The Greeks thought that atoms were the smallest possible particles, and therefore could not be divided. But toward the end of the nineteenth century, physicists began to realize that this might not be true.

Discovery of Electrons

First, physicists discovered a particle much smaller than even the smallest atom. In 1897, British physicist Joseph John Thomson (1856–1940) fused two metal terminals into the ends of a glass tube out of which most of the air had been removed, then passed an electrical current between the two terminals. With a strong enough vacuum in the tube, a bright green glow appeared next to the positive terminal. When Thomson placed a magnet next to the positive terminal, he could make the green glow move.

That green glow, and the magnet's effect on it, indicated to Thomson that electricity was actually

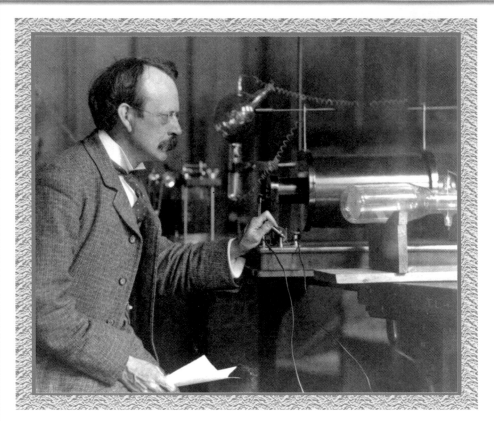

Joseph John Thomson is pictured here in the late nineteenth century experimenting with cathode rays in the Cavendish Laboratory at Cambridge University in England. During his experiments, Thomson tried to determine the basic properties of particles. In 1897, he measured the ratio of the mass of a particle to its electric charge.

the movement of tiny discrete particles, each with a negative electrical charge. Thomson was able to show that each of these particles (which were eventually called electrons) had a mass of around 10^{-30} kilograms. That's about 1/1800 of the mass of the smallest known atom, that of hydrogen.

In the course of his experiments, Thomson noticed that the mass of the electron was the same no matter what material was used in the cathode, or negative terminal, out of which the electrons came. That indicated to him that all atoms, no matter what element they belonged to, must contain electrons. Atoms, in other words, were no longer the smallest possible particle. Instead, they contained even smaller particles within them.

In 1898, Thomson suggested a possible model of the atom. He thought it might consist of negatively charged electrons distributed around a kind of diffuse sphere of positive electricity. This became known as the currant bun or plum pudding model of the atom—the electrons were the currants or plums, and the positive charge was the bun or the pudding.

The Planetary Model of the Atom

The currant bun model of the atom didn't hold up for very long. Scientists studying radioactivity had realized that, like electricity, it, too, consisted of streams of particles. Three types of radioactivity were recognized:

Ernest Rutherford

Ernest Rutherford (1871–1937) was born in New Zealand, but spent his professional life primarily in England. In addition to identifying and naming alpha, beta, and gamma rays and coming up with the planetary model of the atom, Rutherford produced the first artificially induced nuclear reaction in 1919, inspiring much of the later work that eventually led to nuclear power (and nuclear weapons). The rutherford, a unit of radioactivity, is named in his honor.

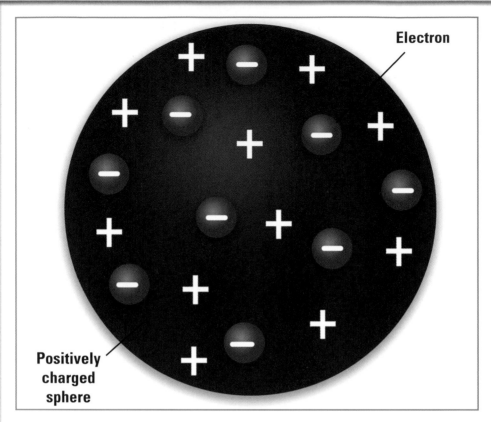

Thomson believed that an atom consisted of a diffuse sphere of positive electricity in which negatively charged electrons were embedded, a model that became known as the currant bun or plum pudding model of the atom.

alpha rays, beta rays, and gamma rays. Moreover, one of the scientists, Ernest Rutherford (1871–1937), who had studied with Thomson, and his assistant, Frederick Soddy (1877–1956), had suggested that radioactivity from substances such as uranium or radium was the result of atoms of the substances spontaneously transforming into atoms of a different kind, releasing radioactive particles in the process.

This transformation of atoms from one kind to another, together with the release of particles, provided another indication that the atom was not indestructible. Rutherford and Soddy's new under-standing of radioactivity also provided a different way to study the inside of atoms and to see if they really did look like currant buns. By firing a stream of particles at a target (a thin gold film) and then studying how that stream of particles was deflected by the target's atoms, you could make an educated guess about the structure of those atoms.

The results were not at all what was expected. If atoms were like currant buns, then the massive alpha particles should have gone right through them, deflected only slightly. Instead, although most of the alpha rays went right through the gold

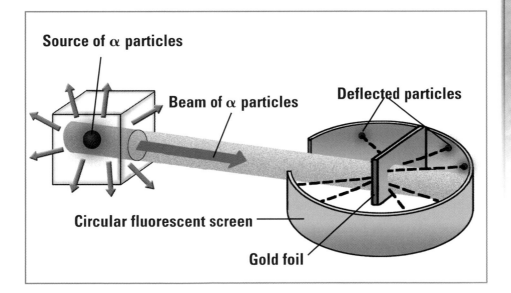

Source of α particles

Beam of α particles

Deflected particles

Circular fluorescent screen

Gold foil

Ernest Rutherford studied atoms with high-speed particles emitted by uranium. These particles were later named alpha (α) particles. When Rutherford directed a beam of the particles at a thin sheet of gold foil, he noticed that although most of it passed through the foil, the beam was detected by the foil. He believed that this deflection could only be explained if all the positive charge of the gold atoms was concentrated in the center, or nucleus.

film, some were deflected quite a bit. Even more unexpectedly, some of the alpha rays actually bounced back. Rutherford said later that it was as astonishing as if a naval shell had bounced off a sheet of tissue paper.

Rutherford realized that the currant bun model of the atom could not be correct. The only way the gold atoms could substantially deflect the alpha rays was if the positive charge in the gold atoms was concentrated at the center of the atom instead of being spread out.

And so the currant bun model of the atom gave way to the solar system model. Just like the solar system consists mostly of empty space, with most of its mass concentrated in the central Sun, around which the much-less-massive planets orbit, so the atom was thought to be mostly empty space, with most of its mass concentrated in a tiny, positively charged central nucleus, orbited by the much-less-massive (and even tinier) negatively charged electrons.

Problems with the New Model

The new solar system model of the atom solved some problems faced by physicists, but at the same time it posed new ones. Electrons orbiting the nucleus of an atom must be constantly changing their direction of motion. Everything that was known about electromagnetic theory at the time stated that whenever an electron changed direction,

For his experiments, Rutherford used alpha particles because from any given radioactive source they have the same energy. Rutherford's model of the atom is sometimes called the planetary model or the solar system model. In his model, a positively charged nucleus is surrounded by a lot of empty space through which the negatively charged electrons move.

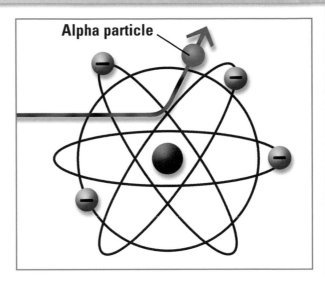

Alpha particle

it should radiate away some of its energy. That loss of energy, in turn, would slow the electrons, so that they should be pulled closer and closer to the nucleus. The only possible outcome would be the complete collapse of the atom. Because atoms are so small, this collapse should occur very quickly—in less than a millionth of a second.

Obviously atoms don't collapse, because if they did, neither atoms nor we, nor our planet, nor our universe would exist. Yet here we are.

There had to be an explanation, and indeed there was one. But that explanation, when it came, continued the collapse of classical physics and hastened the acceptance of what would become known as quantum physics.

3 The Ultraviolet Catastrophe

At about the same time that scientists were beginning to suspect that atoms were not nearly as indivisible as they had thought, they were also beginning to suspect that something wasn't quite right with their understanding of electromagnetic radiation. One of the advances of nineteenth-century science was something called statistical physics. This branch of physics attempts to deal with very complicated systems: a volume of gas, for instance. There are so many atoms in any measurable body of gas, each with its individual motion, that it is impossible to precisely track or predict the action of every atom. Nevertheless, you can both track and predict the action of the gas as a whole fairly accurately. This is because even though there are an enormous number of possible actions the atoms can take, some actions are much more probable than others. The most probable action is performed by such a large majority of atoms that, effectively, the entire volume of gas follows that action.

The Blackbody Problem

In 1900, English physicist Lord Rayleigh (1842–1919) attempted to apply statistical physics to another complex system, the distribution of different frequencies in blackbody radiation, and discovered that classical physics could not accurately predict the distribution of those frequencies.

A blackbody is an object that first perfectly absorbs all the radiation falling on it,

Lord Rayleigh, studied a wide range of subjects in physics, including sound, light, thermodynamics, electromagnetism, and mechanics. Rayleigh's research on the distribution of frequencies in blackbody radiation led to the development of Max Planck's theories on quanta.

then perfectly reemits it all. Although there's no way to build a true blackbody, physicists could approximate one using a special oven. Essentially, this oven was an empty box containing electromagnetic energy.

Obviously, in such an oven, there had to be some sort of equilibrium. If there were more energy in the walls than in the interior, energy would move from the

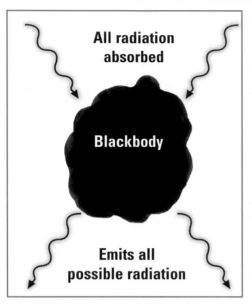

**All radiation
absorbed**

Blackbody

**Emits all
possible radiation**

A blackbody is a body that entirely absorbs all the electromagnetic radiation falling on it, then entirely re-emits it. Blackbody radiation is the electromagnetic radiation that would be radiated from an ideal blackbody. In 1900, Max Planck came up with a mathematical relationship called Planck's radiation law that expresses the distribution of energy in the radiated spectrum of an ideal blackbody.

walls to the interior. If there were more energy in the interior than in the walls, energy would move from the interior to the walls. That meant that both the walls and the interior of the box should have a comparable amount of energy, and should be the same temperature.

It was easy enough to build the special oven and to look inside it to measure the frequencies of the electromagnetic waves inside it.

Scientists knew those frequencies would be limited by the size of the box. In other words, the waves had to fit inside the box. The lowest possible frequency would be one at which the wavelength exactly fit inside the box. After that, you could have twice the lowest frequency (called the second harmonic), then three times the lowest frequency (the third harmonic), and so on to infinity (the millionth billionth trillionth harmonic—and beyond).

According to what was understood about electromagnetic waves at the end of the nineteenth century, each wave carried an energy that was proportional to its frequency and to its amplitude. Even the millionth billionth trillionth harmonic would carry some share of the overall energy of the wave. But if you could have an infinite number of harmonics, and each carried some energy, then the total amount of energy carried by the wave was also infinite—and most of the energy would be carried by extremely high frequencies. If you built a special oven to approximate blackbody radiation, then, according to classical physics, that box would contain an infinite amount of energy. But when physicists built such ovens and looked inside to see how much electromagnetic energy they contained and at what frequencies, the ovens clearly did not contain an infinite amount of energy. (If they had, we'd be using them as power sources.)

These extremely high frequencies of electromagnetic radiation, higher than those of visible light, are collectively called ultraviolet, because they lie "ultra" (Latin for "beyond") the violet end of the visible spectrum. As a result, the inability to accurately predict the distribution of different frequencies in black-body radiation became known as the "ultraviolet catastrophe"—catastrophe, because it represented a huge failure of classical physics.

There seemed to be no way in which classical physics could be modified to predict what was really seen in blackbody radiation experiments. You couldn't divide the observed amount of energy among the infinite number of harmonics, because then you would end up with an infinitely small amount of

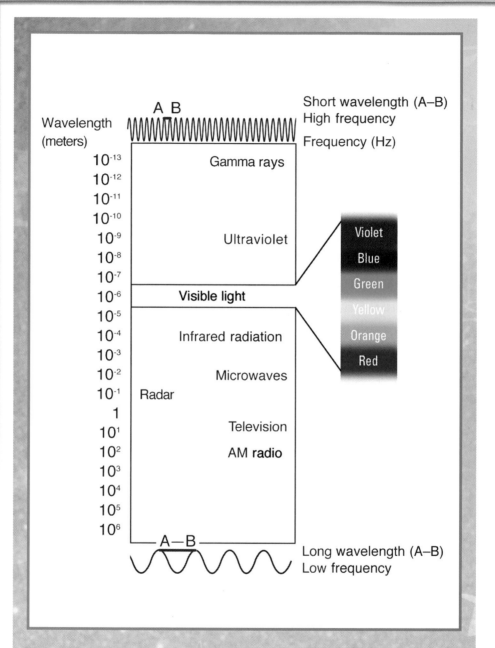

This illustration depicts the electromagnetic spectrum. When the radiated energy's wavelength is short, the frequency is high, and when the wavelength is long, the frequency is low. Gamma rays, for example, have very short wavelengths and a high frequency. AM radio wavelengths are much longer and have a low frequency. The part of the electromagnetic spectrum that is visible to the human eye is called light. Each color of light has a specific wavelength.

energy—essentially nothing—being carried by each frequency. Nor could you give each of the infinite number of possible frequencies a little bit of energy, because then you would end up with infinite energy inside the box. What you really got inside the box was a progression of frequencies similar to those that blacksmiths saw every time they heated up metal for working. As the temperature increased, the inside of the box began to glow in different colors, first orange-red, then a brighter yellow, and finally a hot blue-white. Untroubled by the theoretical concerns of physicists, the real world, it seemed, knew exactly how to divide up energy among the various electromagnetic frequencies available inside a box. Not only that, the real world preferred certain frequencies to others.

The Birth of Quantum Theory

In 1900, the same year Rayleigh discovered the ultraviolet catastrophe, Max Planck, then professor of theoretical physics at the University of Berlin, figured out a way to explain the real world's preference for certain frequencies to others in blackbody radiation. Not only did his solution avoid the ultraviolet catastrophe, but it also gave birth to a whole new kind of physics.

In classical physics, physicists thought that radiation oozed continuously in and out of a blackbody (or in and out of the walls of the special oven used to approximate a blackbody). Planck suggested radiation

Max Planck

Max Planck (1858–1947) was professor of physics at the University of Berlin from 1889 until 1928. His development of quantum theory earned him the 1918 Nobel Prize in Physics. In 1930, Planck was elected president of the Kaiser Wilhelm Society for the Advancement of Science. In the 1930s he criticized the Nazi regime and was forced out of the society, but became president again after World War II (1939–1945). The society was later renamed the Max Planck Society.

German physicist Max Planck is pictured sitting at his desk in 1919. Planck's work in electromagnetic radiation, which later became known as quantum theory, marked a turning point in the history of physics.

might instead be emitted or absorbed in packets of energy of a definite size. He called these packets of energy quanta.

What gave rise to the ultraviolet catastrophe was the need for each electromagnetic wave, no matter how tiny its wavelength, to carry some portion of the overall energy. Planck suggested instead that there must be some absolute minimum amount of energy, proportional to the wave's frequency, carried by each quantum. The energy carried by an electromagnetic wave would therefore have to be a multiple of that minimum. To be more precise, it would be a whole number times the wave's frequency, multiplied by a conversion factor that Planck calculated and that has become known as Planck's constant. It's approximately 6.6 x 10^{-34} joule-seconds, and is represented by the symbol h.

Mathematically, Planck said that an individual atom vibrating at a particular frequency (represented by the Greek letter v) could emit energy only in multiples of hv. It could emit energy of $1hv$, $2hv$, $3hv$, etc., but nothing less than hv and no fractional multiples of hv.

Planck's proposal avoided the ultraviolet catastrophe by making the energy content of the electromagnetic waves inside the special blackbody oven finite instead of potentially infinite. The very high-frequency waves—the trillionth harmonic, and so on—never arose, because the minimum amount of energy required for them to exist exceeded the total amount of energy in the box.

Max Planck's use of the word "quanta" to define the packets of energy within electromagnetic waves provided the name for the new physics that would dominate the twentieth century as classical physics had dominated the nineteenth. The new physics became known as quantum physics.

Sometimes scientists who make great discoveries don't realize what they've done. That wasn't the case with Planck; he told his son that he believed he had made a discovery as significant as those of Newton. It may have sounded like bragging at the time, but he was exactly right.

Uncertainty Over Quantum Theory's Importance

However, the importance of Planck's discovery wasn't immediately apparent. At first, scientists weren't sure what to make of Planck's idea. While it avoided the ultraviolet catastrophe, they weren't certain if it had any other practical use. Even if energy did come in discrete little packages, did that matter? After all, rain comes in drops, but once those drops have joined together in a stream or a lake, you don't need to worry about their singularity anymore.

In 1905, though, a young man working as a third-class examiner in the patent office in Bern, Switzerland, realized that Planck's quanta also

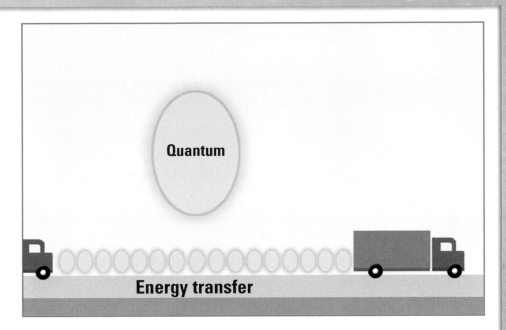

Planck proposed that energy at the subatomic level is transferred in packages or units called quanta. A quantum is the smallest discrete quantity of some physical property that a system can possess.

provided the solution to another problem that seemed to have no solution in classical physics. And in solving that problem, he contributed to the cementing of quantum physics as the new foundation for understanding the universe at its most basic level.

4 The Photoelectric Effect

The young patent clerk's name was Albert Einstein, and the problem he solved in 1905 was the inability of physics to explain the details of a phenomenon called the photoelectric effect.

For several years, physicists had known that under certain conditions, a metal releases electrons when a light shines on it. This phenomenon, called the photoelectric effect, didn't seem particularly surprising, in and of itself. Light is a form of electromagnetic energy. According to classical physics, it made sense that some of that energy could be transferred to the electrons in the metal. (Electrons had recently been discovered by Joseph John Thomson, as you'll recall.) That transfer of energy could conceivably cause the electrons to move faster, to the point where they could escape from the metal altogether.

The number of electrons released could be determined by measuring the electrical current flowing through a wire connected to the metal. The amount of kinetic energy the electrons carried could be measured by the force (in the form of an

electrical charge applied to the metal) that was needed to stop them from moving.

Lenard's Photoelectric Experiments

In 1902, a German physicist named Philipp Lenard (1862–1947) discovered various important properties of the photoelectric effect. First, he discovered that the greater the intensity of the incoming light, the greater the number of electrons that were released. That observation made sense. After all, when bigger, more powerful waves start hitting an ocean beach, they dislodge more sand than smaller, weaker waves.

But Lenard's next discovery did not make sense at all in the world of classical physics. He discovered that the kinetic energy contained in each of the escaping electrons did not increase when the intensity of the light increased. In beach terms, more sand was being dislodged, but no more violently by the more powerful waves than sand was by the weaker waves. In other words, even though the light wave was carrying more energy, none of that energy was being used to speed up the electrons. According to the laws of thermodynamics, energy couldn't be created or destroyed. So where was that extra energy going?

Then Lenard discovered something else. Although increasing the intensity of the light didn't increase the kinetic energy of the escaping electrons, increasing the frequency of the light did. It was as if little, fast-moving waves were able to dislodge sand from a beach more violently than slower-moving giant waves, which isn't what happens. In fact, below a certain frequency, no electrons were dislodged from the metal no matter how intense the light was. Contrarily, electrons above a certain frequency were dislodged from the metal no matter how weak the light was.

Different metals required different frequencies of light to exhibit the photoelectric effect. Green light—low-frequency light—could expel electrons from sodium metal. To produce electrons from copper or aluminum, however, you needed high-frequency ultraviolet light.

Lenard's Equation

Lenard's investigation of the photoelectric effect produced this basic equation:

$$1/2mv^2 = hv - K$$

In this equation, m is the mass of an escaping electron; v is its velocity; $1/2mv^2$ is the standard formula used to calculate kinetic energy, v is the frequency of the light wave, h is Planck's constant (6.6×10^{-34} joule-seconds), and K is a number that varies from metal to metal.

Einstein's Breakthrough

No one starting from the assumption that light is a wave could make sense of Lenard's findings. Einstein's breakthrough was to realize that Planck's idea of energy packets, or quanta, could be used to quite neatly explain the photoelectric effect.

If light consisted of a stream of quanta instead of

Albert Einstein

Albert Einstein (1879–1955), probably the best-known scientist of the twentieth century, did not talk until he was three. However, even as a youth, he showed great mathematical ability.

Einstein dropped out of school for a year when he was fifteen. He eventually attended the Swiss Federal Institute of Technology, but often cut classes; he passed by studying a classmate's notes. His professors refused to recommend him for an academic position—which is why he was working in the patent office in Bern, Switzerland, in 1905.

In 1905, Albert Einstein, pictured here in March 1953, published a theory on the photoelectric effect. He believed that light and other forms of radiation are made up of discrete bundles of energy and that the energy of each bundle depends on the light's frequency.

being a continuous wave, then an electron would be ejected from the metal because one of these quanta had hit it. In the process, the quanta would transfer all its energy to the electron.

In Planck's theory, the amount of energy in each quantum of light was directly proportional to the frequency of the light. This hypothesis meant that if the frequency were too low, the quantum of light would not be carrying enough energy to dislodge any electron it happened to hit. That neatly explained why no electrons were produced below a certain critical frequency, differing from metal to metal, no matter how intense the light beam might be.

Raising the frequency would increase the energy carried by each quantum. Once the frequency was high enough for the quanta to carry enough energy to dislodge electrons, increasing the frequency would also increase the energy imparted to the electrons. That increase in energy would impart a higher velocity to the dislodged electrons.

In Einstein's theory, increasing the intensity of the light beam wouldn't increase the energy available to dislodge electrons. Instead, it would simply increase the number of quanta present in the light beam. The increase in quanta would increase the overall number of electrons produced by making it more likely that quanta of light would collide with electrons. However, the increase in quanta would have no effect on the velocity of the ejected electrons.

Einstein's Equation

These quanta of light became known as photons. In Einstein's theory of light, the energy carried by each photon is entirely determined by the frequency, expressed by: $E=h\nu$, where E is energy, h is Planck's constant, and ν is the frequency of the light.

The reason we don't ordinarily notice that light is made up of individual photons instead of smooth, continuous waves, is that the amount of energy carried by individual photons is extremely tiny.

Experiments by American physicist Robert A. Millikan (1868–1953) in 1915 verified Einstein's theory. In 1921, Einstein was awarded the Nobel Prize in Physics for his work on the photoelectric effect (not for his theory of relativity, as most people suppose).

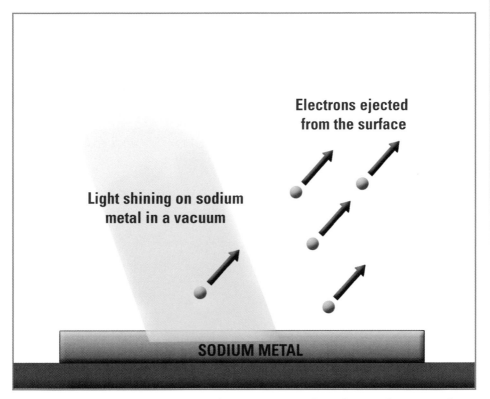

When electromagnetic radiation shines on a metal, such as sodium metal, the surface of the metal releases energized electrons. This is called the photoelectric effect. The way these electrons are released contradicts the classical theories of electromagnetic radiation behaving like a wave and supports the quantum view in which electromagnetic radiation is treated as being made up of particles.

Light: Both Wave and Particle?

Einstein's theory left physicists (including Einstein) more than a little uneasy. In the nineteenth century, experiments and mathematical theory alike seemed to have established that light behaved like a wave. Now Einstein said it was really made up of particles. Could both theories be correct? It seemed impossible, and yet it also seemed to be true. Young and Maxwell had shown that light was a wave; Planck and Einstein had shown that it was made up of quanta, or particles. Getting a firm intellectual grasp on this apparently contradictory notion became the most pressing task of physicists in the early part of the twentieth century.

Line Spectra

Spectroscopy began with Sir Isaac Newton, who first realized that the white light of the Sun could be broken into the colors of the rainbow by passing it through a glass prism. He used the word "spectrum" to describe this phenomenon.

Fraunhofer's Lines

In 1814, German physicist Joseph von Fraunhofer (1787–1826) discovered that if the Sun's spectrum was spread widely enough, it was crossed by a large number of fine dark lines. These lines are now known as Fraunhofer lines. To create his spectra, Fraunhofer pioneered the use of the diffraction grating. The use of the diffraction grating was an extension of Young's experiments that had demonstrated the wave nature of light. A diffraction grating is an array of very fine slits in an opaque screen, or a screen of fine wires very close together. Light passing through the slits or between the wires produces interference patterns, just as in Young's experiment, but these patterns made by the diffraction grating show the colors of

Joseph von Fraunhofer (standing at center) demonstrated his device,
called a spectrometer, to his German colleagues circa 1820. Fraunhofer
built the first diffraction grating, which was made up of 260 parallel
wires. He used the grating to closely study the Sun's spectrum, discover-
ing that it was crossed with dark lines.

the spectrum. Diffraction grating of various types
continues to be used in spectroscopy today.

As the nineteenth century progressed, scientists
studied the spectra produced by light sources such
as flames, electrical arcs, and sparks. Within the
spectra of these light sources were bright lines.
Then, in 1848, the French physicist Jean-Bernard-
Leon Foucault (1819–1868) discovered that a flame
containing sodium would absorb yellow light coming
from a strong electrical arc placed behind it.

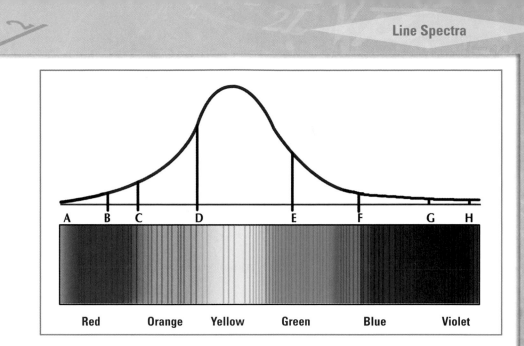

The dark lines that Fraunhofer observed in 1814 while studying the spectrum of sunlight are now called Fraunhofer lines. The most important lines he labeled with capital letters, beginning at the red end of the spectrum. Lines A through H are pictured here.

Kirchhoff's Discovery

In 1859, Gustav Kirchhoff (1824–1887) showed that each element, when heated until it was incandescent, produced a characteristic pattern of bright lines. This pattern meant you could determine the chemical makeup of a light source by studying its spectrum. (Kirchhoff was aided in this discovery by fellow German Robert Bunsen, inventor of the Bunsen burner.) Kirchhoff also concluded that the dark lines Fraunhofer had seen were the result of elements at the surface of the Sun absorbing part of the continuous spectrum of light emitted from the much hotter interior. Since Fraunhofer lines indicated which elements were present at the Sun's surface, you could use them to analyze the atmosphere of the Sun.

Similarly, you could use spectroscopy to analyze the chemical makeup of distant stars. Astronomers quickly set about to conduct such analyses, even though no one had a good explanation for *why* there should be distinct spectral lines for each element. According to classical physics, there was no reason why a heated element shouldn't produce a continuous spectrum. One spectrum that was frequently observed was the spectrum of hydrogen, because it is the most abundant element in the universe.

The Balmer Equation

In 1885, a Swiss schoolmaster named Johann Jakob Balmer (1825–1898), by carefully studying the hydrogen spectrum, came up with a simple, accurate formula $1/\lambda = R(1/2^2 - 1/n^2)$ where λ is the wavelength at which the visible lines in the spectrum of hydrogen appear, R is a constant, and n is simply an integer that described the wavelengths of hydrogen's four visible spectral lines. In a way, this was the first hint of quantum physics, though no one recognized it at the time. Further experimentation by other scientists showed that Balmer's equation also predicted the location of other spectral lines in the hydrogen spectrum outside of the range of visible light. The explanation for the Balmer equation came almost thirty years after it was formulated, from a young Danish scientist named Niels Bohr.

By 1912, Bohr was considering various problems with the new planetary model of the atom, including its inability to explain line spectra. He was familiar with Planck's finding that energy could come in discrete packets, or quanta, instead of continuous waves. He also knew about Einstein's photons, another example of quanta.

Bohr's Quantum Atom

In 1913, Bohr suggested extending these new quantum ideas to the atom. Bohr suggested, first, that for some reason (as yet unknown) the electrons orbiting the nucleus of an atom did not radiate energy, even though Maxwell's equations governing electromagnetic radiation said they should. (Remember that if they did radiate energy, they would quickly lose enough energy to collapse into the nucleus, and the universe as we know it couldn't exist.) Instead, Bohr suggested, electrons can move around the nucleus of an atom in stable orbits with no loss of energy—but not in any conceivable orbit. Bohr said electrons were limited to

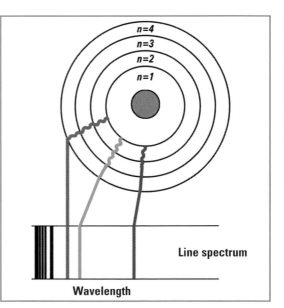

In Bohr's explanation of line spectra, electrons can only occupy certain orbits around the nucleus. In Bohr's model, when an atom of a gas released energy (in the form of a photon), an electron would move down to a lower orbit that required less energy, and when an atom acquired energy, an electron would move up to a higher energy level.

Line spectrum

Wavelength

41

Niels Bohr

Danish physicist Niels Bohr (1885–1962) received the Nobel Prize in Physics in 1922, for his model of the atom. He went on to make many other major contributions to theoretical physics. After fleeing German-occupied Denmark during World War II, Bohr made his way to the United States, where he helped develop the first atomic bomb. After the war, he returned to Denmark to work on peaceful uses for atomic energy. The chemical element with the atomic number 107 is named bohrium in his honor.

a very few specific orbits. The reason, he said, was that the amount of angular momentum, or spin, that the electrons could have as they circled the nucleus had to be a whole-number multiple of some basic unit. In classical physics terms, none of this explanation made any sense. If the atom were really structured like the solar system, then a vast number of orbits should have been possible, and so should any amount of spin.

Photons from Jumping Electrons

Bohr pointed out that for an electron to jump from one stable orbit to another—to increase or decrease its spin—it had to either gain or lose energy. If an electron loses spin and drops to a lower orbit, he said, it ejects energy in the form of a photon.

The usual way for an electron to gain energy would be via a collision with another particle. Collisions became more likely when substances were heated, because the atoms in the substance would then vibrate more rapidly. Occasionally such a collision would give an electron some extra energy, enough to make it jump to a higher orbit. After a while, however, it would slip back down to its regular orbit, and in doing so, it would eject a photon.

Once an electron had reached its lowest possible orbit, no more energy could be lost. Unlike Rutherford's original planetary model of the atom, Bohr's model could explain why atoms don't collapse.

Bohr was able to calculate what the frequency of the radiation ejected by an electron jumping from a higher stable orbit to a lower one should be in heated hydrogen. That frequency matched up precisely with the Balmer formula. The sharp spectral lines seen from heated hydrogen were the result of photons of specific frequencies being ejected from electrons as they dropped from a higher to a lower stable orbit.

Planck first suggested that energy could come in discrete packets, which he called quanta; Einstein applied his idea to light, and deduced the photon; Bohr took their ideas and applied them to the model of the atom, and changed science's understanding of the basic building block of the physical world. Together, they gave birth to a whole new branch of science: quantum physics.

Glossary

atoms (AH-temz) The smallest possible unit of an element, consisting of a nucleus surrounded by orbiting electrons.

electron (ih-LEK-trahn) A negatively charged particle that is one of the basic constituents of the atom.

frequency (FREE-kwen-see) The number of wave crests (or troughs) that pass a given point in a given amount of time.

kinetic energy (keh-NEH-tik EH-ner-jee) The energy of motion.

mass (MAS) A basic property of all physical objects that causes them to have weight in a gravitational field.

nucleus (NOO-klee-es) The central part of an atom, around which electrons orbit.

photoelectric effect (foh-toh-ih-LEK-trik ih-FEKT) The release of electrons caused by light shining on metal.

photon (FOH-tahn) A particle of light.

quantum (pl., quanta) (KWAN-tem) (pl. quanta [KWAN-teh]) A tiny, discrete packet of energy.

spectrum (spek-TREM) The series of colors produced by shining a beam of light through a prism or diffraction grating.

subatomic (sub-eh-TAH-mik) Having to do with particles smaller than the atom.

vacuum (VAK-yoom) A space absolutely devoid of matter.

velocity (veh-LAH-seh-tee) The speed at which an object is moving in a particular direction.

wavelength (WAYV-lenkth) In a series of waves, the distance between one wave crest (or trough) and the next.

For More Information

American Institute of Physics
One Physics Ellipse
College Park, MD 20740-3843
(301) 209-3100
Web site: http//www.aip.org

American Physical Society
One Physics Ellipse
College Park, MD 20740-3844
(301) 209-3200
Web site: http://www.aps.org

Fermilab
P.O. Box 500
Batavia, IL 60510-0500
(630) 840-3000
Web site: http://www.fnal.gov

Web Sites

Due to the changing nature of Internet links, the Rosen
Publishing Group, Inc., has developed an online list of Web
sites related to the subject of this book. This site is updated
regularly. Please use this link to access the list:

http://www.rosenlinks.com/liph/baqp

For Further Reading

Fleisher, Paul. *Relativity and Quantum Mechanics: Principles of Modern Physics.* Minneapolis, MN: Lerner Publications Co., 2001.

Polkinghorne, John. *Quantum Theory: A Very Short Introduction.* New York: Oxford University Press, 2002.

Stwertka, Alberta. *World of Atoms & Quarks.* Breckenridge, CO: 21st Century Books, 1997.

Topp, Patricia. *This Strange Quantum World and You.* Nevada City, CA: Blue Dolphin Publishing, 1999.

Bibliography

Kuhn, Karl F. *Basic Physics: A Self-Teaching Guide, Second Edition*, New York: John Wiley & Sons, Inc., 1996.

Lightman, Alan. *Great Ideas in Physics.* New York: McGraw-Hill, 2000.

Lindley, David. *Where Does the Weirdness Go?* New York: Basic Books, 1996.

Polkinghorne, John. *Quantum Theory: A Very Short Introduction.* New York: Oxford University Press, 2002.

Taylor, John G. *New Worlds in Physics.* London, England: Faber and Faber, 1974.

Index

About the Author

Edward Willett writes a weekly science column for newspaper and radio and is the author of more than twenty books on a variety of science, health, and computer topics, for both children and adults. He also writes science fiction and fantasy, and is a professional actor and singer. He lives with his wife and daughter in Regina, Saskatchewan, Canada.

Photo Credits

Cover © David Parker/Science Photo Library; p. 5 © Genevieve Leaper; Ecoscene/Corbis; p. 7 © Jim Sugar/Corbis; pp. 8, 10, 16, 17, 19, 22, 24, 29, 35, 39, 41 by Geri Fletcher; p. 14 © University of Cavendish Laboratory of the Braun EIM Tube; p. 21 Library of Congress, Prints and Photographs Division; p. 26 © Bettmann/Corbis; p. 33 © Esther Bubley/Getty Images; p. 38 © Hulton/Archive/Getty Images.

Designer: Tahara Anderson; **Editor:** Kathy Kuhtz Campbell